LIFE OF ST. HILDEFONSUS

LIFE OF ST. HILDEFONSUS

RODERIC OF CERRAT

Copyright 2006 by Dalcassian Press

All rights reserved. No part of this book may be reproduced in any manner whatsoever without written permission except in the case of brief quotations embodied in critical articles and reviews.

No part of this publication may be reproduced, distributed, or transmitted in any form or by any means, including photocopying, recording, or other electronic or mechanical methods, without the prior written permission of the publisher, except in the case of brief quotations embodied in critical reviews and certain other non-commercial uses permitted by copyright law. For permission requests, write to Dalcassian Press at admin@thescriptoriumproject.com

Translator: Curtin, D.P. (1985-)

ISBN: 979-8-3305-9190-9 (Paperback)
ISBN: 979-8-3493-8121-8 (eBook)
Library of Congress Control Number:

Printed by Ingram Content Group, 1 Ingram Blvd, La Vergne, Tennessee
First Printing 2006, Dalcassian Press, Wilmington, DE

This work is part of a series produced in association with the Scriptorium Project and its community of scholars and translators.
Please visit our website at: www.thescriptoriumproject.com

INTRODUCTION

St. Ildefonsus of Toledo, a 7th-century bishop and theologian, remains a towering figure in the history of early medieval Christianity, particularly in the Visigothic Kingdom of Hispania. Born into a noble family around 607 AD in Toledo, Ildefonsus devoted his life to monasticism, ecclesiastical reform, and theological writing, becoming a central voice in the defense of Marian doctrines. As a monk, abbot, and eventually archbishop of Toledo, his legacy profoundly shaped the liturgical, theological, and cultural landscape of the Iberian Peninsula. Revered both during his life and after his death, St. Ildefonsus's contributions to Christian doctrine and devotion continue to resonate in the Catholic tradition.

Born into a Visigothic noble family, Ildefonsus received a strong classical and religious education in Toledo, a city that served as both a political and ecclesiastical capital of the Visigothic Kingdom. He entered the monastery of Agali, located outside Toledo, against the wishes of his family, indicating his deep personal commitment to the religious life. There, he advanced quickly due to his learning and piety, becoming abbot by 650 AD. His years in monastic life were marked by a strong adherence to ascetic principles and theological study. Ildefonsus emphasized the importance of discipline and intellectual rigor, and he helped elevate the status of monasticism in Spain. During this period, he wrote extensively, gaining recognition for his learning and devotion to the Virgin Mary, which would later define his theological legacy.

Ildefonsus was appointed Archbishop of Toledo in 657 AD, succeeding Bishop Eugenius II. His elevation came not just from his ecclesiastical rank but from the high regard in which he was held throughout the Spanish Church. As archbishop, he played a critical role in church politics, liturgical reform, and the consolidation of orthodoxy in the face of lingering Arian influences that had once permeated Visigothic Spain. Toledo, as the metropolitan see, held great religious influence, and Ildefonsus used his position to bolster the authority of the Church. He worked closely with the Visigothic kings, notably King Recceswinth, and contributed to a period of relative religious unity and stability. His tenure helped secure Toledo's primacy over other Iberian sees and helped unify the liturgical practices across the kingdom.

St. Ildefonsus is perhaps best known for his fervent devotion to the Virgin Mary and his theological works that articulated and defended her perpetual virginity and special place in salvation history. His most famous work, *De Virginitate Sanctae Mariae contra tres infideles* ("On the Virginity of Holy Mary against Three Infidels"), was a robust defense of Marian doctrine, written in response to heretical views that questioned her perpetual virginity. This treatise not only addressed theological challenges of his time but also contributed to the growing cult of the Virgin in Western Christianity. It established Ildefonsus as one of the earliest Western theologians to place such strong emphasis on Marian devotion, influencing later figures such as St. Anselm and the writers of the Roman Missal. The legend surrounding Ildefonsus's devotion to Mary adds to his mystique and sanctity. According to tradition, the Virgin Mary appeared to him in the cathedral of Toledo and presented him with a chasuble (liturgical vestment) as a reward for his writings in her honor. This miraculous event reportedly took place on December 18, which became a major Marian feast day in Toledo and in other parts of Spain.

In addition to his Marian works, Ildefonsus wrote several other theological and ecclesiastical texts. Among them is *De Cognitione Baptismi*, which addresses baptismal theology, and *De Progressu Spiritualis Deserti*, a spiritual treatise on the monastic path to holiness. His writings exhibit clarity, deep scriptural grounding, and a pastoral sensitivity that made them accessible and influential in monastic and ecclesiastical circles alike. Ildefonsus's Latin style was marked by both classical and biblical influences, reflecting his education and his desire to link Christian teaching with a more refined cultural expression. His work became a model for later Visigothic writers and for the development of Christian Latin literature in Spain.

St. Ildefonsus died on January 23, 667 AD, and was quickly venerated as a saint. His tomb in Toledo became a pilgrimage site, and his feast day is still celebrated in the Catholic Church, particularly in Spain, on January 23. The cathedral of Toledo, one of the most significant religious centers in Spain, continues to honor his legacy through liturgy and art. Throughout the Middle Ages, Ildefonsus was regarded as a spiritual patron of the Spanish Church. His emphasis on Marian devotion helped cement Mary's role as a central figure in Spanish Catholicism. His liturgical reforms contributed to the Mozarabic Rite, a unique Spanish liturgical tradition that persisted even after the Islamic conquest of much of the Iberian Peninsula.

St. Ildefonsus stands as one of the most important figures in early Spanish Christianity. His life of monastic discipline, his intellectual vigor, and his theological devotion—especially to the Virgin Mary—earned him a lasting place in the history of the Church. As Archbishop of Toledo, he not only shaped the liturgical and theological direction of the Spanish Church but also inspired generations of Christian thinkers and believers. His legacy continues to be felt today in the enduring reverence for Mary, the celebration of his feast, and the historical memory preserved in the Church he helped to strengthen.

THE LIFE OF ST. HILDEFONSUS

1. Hildefonsus, from Spain, born of noble parents in the city of Toledo, was entrusted to the noble bishop of Toledo, Eugenio, for nurturing. Saint Eugenio, diligently instructing him in good morals and the rudiments of letters, observing his capacity, sent him to the blessed Isidore, archbishop of Seville, where the doctrine of eloquence, the discipline of the arts, and the study of theology flourished so that he taught all who flocked to him according to the capacity of each individual.

2. Therefore, Hildefonsus was kindly received by the blessed Isidore, both for his lineage and for Eugenio, and being subject to his teachings, after having labored greatly in the study of the liberal arts, he devoted himself more diligently to the law of the Lord. With these

and other honorable exercises, always focusing his entire mental affection while still tender in years, he set himself as an example of human life for the young men who studied with him, not only turning them away from illicit activities but also informing them to do good works by adhering to virtue. No one was more diligent in study than he; no one prayed more frequently than he. However, he distinguished between the times for reading and praying in such a way that neither reading impeded prayer nor prayer hindered reading; but that, attentively, he could either read or pray, with the reading being a relief for prayer and prayer a relief for reading. Wherever he went, prayer accompanied him, both going and returning; in secular conversation, there was nothing indecent or dishonorable in him; but as a servant of Christ and an imitator of the saints, he not only progressed in wisdom but also grew remarkably in the increase of virtues.

3. After passing through childhood, when he reached the age that allures with the pleasures of the flesh, wishing to repress illicit impulses, he fortified his body by opposing the contrary qualities of vices with a wall of virtues, so that not only did he not allow entrance to vices, but also access was forbidden unless through the infestation of temptations; for he was permitted to be tempted like other saints, not for the defect of virtues but for the advancement of testing. Out of a spirit of piety, he condescended to the misery of the poor, while not losing the seal of chastity; and offering to God the other ornaments of virtue, he wholly devoted himself to the Lord.

4. Finally leaving secular disciplines, he returned to the blessed Eugenio, and was ordained a deacon by him. However, lest his life, which he had kept immaculate, be stained by the delight of temporal things, he devoted himself to serve God with others who lived there, in the church of Saints Cosmas and Damian, which is located in the suburb of Toledo, which was formerly called the monastery of Agalia. And as he was going to that place, and saw his father pursuing him from afar with rapid fury, so that he might not be defrauded of his purpose,

he hid himself in an old ruin; however, his father, passing by the hiding place, sought the monastery of Agalia with threats, and not finding him, returned. Therefore, when the father returned, he approached the monastery and accepted the habit.

5. After many years had passed, when he was considered second to none in religious life, he became abbot. Thus, as abbot, he organized the affairs of the Church, providing for the needs of all. Observing the morals of all, and attending to the qualities of behavior, he presented himself to each as was necessary, being gentle to the gentle, but having feelings against those who were offended. For the abbot of Agalia was a sword to the offended.

6. In a village that was then called Bisensis, he built a convent for virgins and enriched it with his own resources. However, his fame spread throughout all of Spain, since neither a holier, nor a more trustworthy, nor a more eloquent, nor a more illustrious, nor a more righteous, nor a more knowledgeable person could be found than he. Upon the death of Eugenio, he was brought back to Toledo by the clergy and the people, and the pontiff was substituted while all praised him. Therefore, having become pontiff, he prepared the table of preaching for the quality of each individual.

7. One day, as the feast of Saint Leocadia was approaching, while everyone gathered to celebrate the feast, as Saint Hildefonsus prayed at her tomb on his knees, that sacred virgin presented herself before all those standing there. And when the holy man encountered her presence, as if embracing him, she spoke these words: "By the life of Hildefonsus, my Lady lives." And I believe she spoke these words because, when the faith and truth of the virginity of the blessed Mary had been destroyed and extinguished by the error of unbelievers throughout almost all of Spain, he wrote a book about her virginity, through which that faith, as if dead, revived, and the error was completely destroyed. But in order to leave a memory of the revelation

for posterity, he cut a part of the garment that had covered her living body with the knife of Prince Reccesvind, who was present at the feast, which he placed in silver vessels with those relics; judging it unworthy that he who had cut the holy garment should further tear it as polluted. After these things were done, everyone solemnly celebrated the feast of the Virgin.

8. He greatly loved the Mother of God and honored her with all reverence; in her praise, he composed a distinguished volume in elegant style about her most holy virginity, which pleased the Virgin so much that she appeared to him holding the book in her hand and gave thanks for such a work. He, wishing to honor her more highly, decided that her solemnity, that is, the feast of the Annunciation, should be celebrated every year on the eighth day before the feast of the Nativity of the Lord; so that since the feast of the Annunciation often occurs around the Passion or Resurrection of the Lord, it might be restored on the aforementioned day. And indeed it is quite fitting that at the same time the Annunciation of the Lord should be celebrated before his Nativity, which solemnity is celebrated by many churches in Spain.

9. However, on the imminent day of the feast of the Mother of God, he decided to celebrate litanies with fasting three days prior, so that the feast would be observed more devoutly. Therefore, at midnight of that feast, while he was rising for Matins, and the book of virginity, which he had composed with remarkable eloquence, was ready to be read, in order to fulfill the vigils he had vowed to God and blessed Mary, the ministers who were leading, carrying the lights, opening the doors of the church, saw within the church a heavenly light, which they could not bear in any way and, as if dead, fled with trembling, leaving the lights behind. Hildefonsus, however, undeterred, entered, and when he had bent his knees before the altar in the usual manner, and being well aware, he looked around and saw the queen of virgins sitting in the seat where he used to sit and preach to the people. He also saw the throngs of virgins praising her. And when

the Virgin and the holy man looked at each other, the most holy Virgin said to him: "Because you have remained with a pure mind and firm faith in my praises, and you have depicted my praise in the hearts of the faithful with sweet eloquence, and you have girded your loins with the belt of virginity, I have brought you a garment of perpetual glory, with which you shall be clothed on the day and solemnity of mine; you shall sit in this seat. But if anyone after you presumes to wear this garment and sit in this chair, he will not escape punishment." Having said this, she vanished and left him the garment which we call the Alb. He, leading a blessed life, happily migrated to the Lord.

10. After him, Siargius, having become bishop, said: "Just as I am a man, so I know my predecessor was a man; why should I not be clothed with that which he was clothed, since I perform the same office of bishop?" And when he was clothed with the garment, he was constricted more tightly and fell dead; and terrified, they took the garment and placed it in the treasury of the church.

LATIN TEXT

1. Hildefonsus ex Hispania, civitate Toletana nobilibus parentibus oriundus, nobili Toletanae sedis praesuli Eugenio traditur nutriendus. Quem sanctus Eugenius bonis moribus, et litterarum rudimentis instruens diligenter, capacitatem ejus attendens, ad beatum Isidorum archipraesulem Hispalensem transmisit eum, apud quem omnis eloquentiae doctrina, artium disciplina, Theologiae et speculatio ita vigebat, ut omnes qui ad eum confluebant, pro capacitate singulorum instruebat.

2. Hildefonsus igitur a beato Isidoro et propter genus, et propter Eugenium benigne susceptus, et ejus subjectus dogmatibus, cum in liberalium artium studio plurimum laborasset, in lege Domini studiosius aciem infigebat. His atque aliis exercitiis honestis toto mentis affectu teneris adhuc sub annis semper intendens, adolescentulis qui secum studebant, in exemplum humanae vitae seipsum proponens, non solum ab illicitis revocabat, verum etiam bonis operibus inhaerendo ad bonum operandum informabat. Nullus eo studiosius lectioni instabat, frequentius eo nullus orationi vacabat. Legendi tamen, atque orandi vices inter se sic distinguebat, ut nec lectio impediret orationem, nec oratio lectionem; sed ut attentius vel legeret, vel oraret, illi vicissim relevamen erat orationis lectio, et lectionis oratio. Ubicunque iret eum oratio comitabatur euntem et redeuntem; in saeculari autem conversatione illa nihil indecens, nil inhonestum erat in eo; sed ut servus Christi, et sanctorum imitator, non solum sapientia proficiebat, sed et augmento virtutum mirabiliter crescebat.

3. Transacta autem puerili aetate, cum ad illam cui carnis oblectamenta alludunt veniret aetatem, motus illicitos volens reprimere, corpus suum muro virtutum contrarias earum qualitates contrariis vi-

tiorum qualitatibus opponens, ita circumscripsit, ut non solum vitiis non pateret ingressus, verum etiam nisi per tentationum infestationem interdiceretur accessus; permittebatur enim sicut et caeteri sancti tentari, non ad virtutum defectum, sed ad probationis profectum. Ex affectu autem pietatis miseriae pauperum condescendebat, ex sigillo castitatis virginitatis lilium non amittebat; et caetera virtutum ornamenta Deo offerens, Deo placens, se totum Domino immolabat.

4. Relictis denique saecularibus disciplinis, ad beatum Eugenium reversus, ab eo in diaconum est ordinatus. Ne autem vita sua, quam immaculatam servaverat, delectatione temporalium macularetur, in ecclesia sanctorum Cosmae et Damiani, quae in suburbio sita est Toletano, quae antiquitus Agaliense monasterium dicebatur, relictis parentibus, cum aliis qui habitabant ibi servire Deo devovit. Cumque ad locum praedictum pergeret, et patrem suum rapido furore se persequentem a longe conspiceret, ne a proposito fraudaretur, in vetusta macerie se occultavit; pater vero latibulum praeteriens Agaliense monasterium comminando petiit, et eum non inveniens rediit. Reverso igitur patre, monasterium adiit, et habitum suscepit.

5. Multis annis transactis, cum nulli in religione haberetur secundus, factus est abbas. Factus igitur abbas res Ecclesiae ordinabat, omnibus necessaria ministrabat. Mores omnium circumspiciens, qualitates morum attendens, singulis prout necessarium erat se ipsum exhibebat, mansuetis mansuetus, contra vero offensos offensos habebat affectus. Nam Ensis offensis erat abbas Agaliensis.

6. In villa autem quae tunc Bisensis dicebatur, virginum coenobium aedificavit, et propriis facultatibus ditavit. Fama autem ejus per totam Hispaniam divulgata, cum nec sanctior, nec probabilior, nec eloquentior, nec illustrior, nec rectior, nec scientia perfectior eo inveniri posset, defuncto Eugenio a clero et populo Toletum reducitur, et omnibus eum laudantibus pontifex subrogatur. Factus ergo pontifex

praedicationis mensam pro qualitate singulorum omnibus praeparabat.

7. Quadam die dum sanctae Leocadiae festivitas immineret, dum omnes festivitati celebrandae convenirent, dum sanctus Hildefonsus ad sepulcrum ejus flexis genibus oraret, virgo illa sacra coram omnibus ibi astantibus illi se praesentavit. Cum autem vir sanctus in ejus praesentiam occurreret, ipsa quasi eum amplexans, hujusmodi protulit verba: « Per vitam Hildefonsi vivit Domina mea. » Atque ideo eam haec verba protulisse arbitror, quia cum fides et veritas virginitatis beatae Mariae errore infidelium per totam fere Hispaniam destructa et emortua esset, librum de ejus virginitate scripsit, per quem fides illa quasi mortua revixit, et errorem penitus destruxit. Sed ut memoriam revelationis posteris relinqueret, partem vestimenti quod membra illius viventis texerat, Reccesvindi principis, qui festo intererat, cultro praecidit, quem cum eisdem reliquiis vasculis argenteis condidit; indignum judicans ut qui praeciderat sancta, scinderet ulterius polluta. Quibus peractis omnes festum Virginis solemniter peregerunt.

8. Dei genitricem multum diligebat, et omni reverentia eam honorabat: in cujus laudem volumen insigne eleganti stylo de ejus sanctissima virginitate composuit, quod ita ipsi Virgini placuit, ut librum ipsum manu tenens ei apparuit, et pro tali opere gratias retulit. Ille autem cupiens eam altius honorare, constituit ut celebraretur solemnitas ejus, id est, festum Annuntiationis, singulis annis octavo die ante festum Natalis Domini; ut quia festum Annuntiationis circa Passionem vel Resurrectionem Domini frequenter evenit, in praedicto die restitui possit. Et quidem satis congrue, ut eodem tempore prius Annuntiatio Domini quam ejus Nativitas celebretur, quae solemnitas per multas Ecclesias Hispaniae celebratur.

9. Imminente autem die festivitatis Genitricis Dei, tribus diebus ante, litanias cum jejunio statuit celebrari, ut festum devotius ageretur. Nocte igitur media ipsius festi dum ad Matutinum consurgeret,

et liber virginitatis, quem ipse mira facundia composuerat, ad legendum paratus esset, ut vigilias quas Deo et beatae Mariae voverat expleret, ministri qui praeibant, qui luminaria portabant, ostia ecclesiae aperientes, intra ecclesiam lumen coeleste viderunt, quod nullo modo ferre valentes quasi mortui relictis luminaribus cum tremore fugerunt. Hildefonsus vero imperterritus ingrediens, cum ante altare solito more genua flecteret, et bene conscius circumquaque conspiciens vidit virginum reginam sedentem in sede ubi ipse solebat sedere, et populo praedicare. Vidit et virginum turmas laudantes eam. Cumque Virgo et vir sanctus se mutuo respicerent, ait ei Virgo sanctissima: « Quoniam mente pura, fideque firma, in meis laudibus permansisti, et laudem meam in corda fidelium dulci eloquio depinxisti, et lumbos tuos virginitatis cingulo praecinxisti, de vestimentis perpetuae gloriae vestimentum attuli tibi, quo vestiaris in die et solemnitate mea; in hac sede sedebis. Si quis autem post te praesumpserit hoc vestimentum induere, et in hac cathedra sedere, non carebit ultione. Hisque dictis disparuit, et vestimentum quod nos Albam vocamus, ei reliquit. Ipse autem felicem ducens vitam, feliciter migravit ad Dominum

10. Post quem Siargius episcopus factus ait: Sicut ego sum homo, sic et hominem scio praedecessorem meum; cur non induar eo quo ipse indutus est vestimento, cum eodem fungar praesulatus officio? Qui cum vestimento indutus esset, constrictus arctius, cecidit mortuus; perterritique vestimentum tulerunt, et in thesauro ecclesiae reposuerunt.

This work was produced in association with:

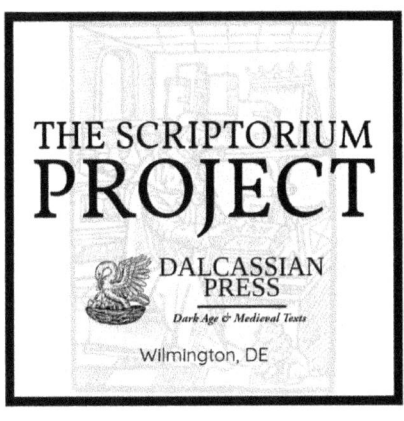

www.ingramcontent.com/pod-product-compliance
Lightning Source LLC
LaVergne TN
LVHW061050070526
838201LV00074B/5248